MIND-BENDING MAZE PUZZLES

LAGOON
BOOKS

Series editor: Heather Dickson
Maze compiler: Adrian Fisher
Additional contributors: Robert Abbott,
Randoll Coate, Scott Kim, Ed Pegg,
Steve Ryan, Gaby Wirminghaus

Published by:
LAGOON BOOKS
PO BOX 311, KT2 5QW, UK

ISBN 1899712720
© LAGOON BOOKS, 1999
Lagoon Books is a trade mark of
Lagoon Trading Company Limited.
All rights reserved.

Printed in Singapore.

MIND-BENDING MAZE PUZZLES

INTRODUCTION

At last. A maze book that even the most obsessive maze enthusiasts will find challenging!

This colourful collection of traditional labyrinths and state-of-the-art mazes with rules has been compiled by Adrian Fisher, the world's leading maze designer, who has been creating indoor and outdoor mazes for more than 20 years.

To date he has created over 135 mazes worldwide, in a variety of materials from turf and hedges to brick pavement, wood, water, mirror and rope. Among his most famous works are his formal hedge mazes at Blenheim Palace and Leeds Castle, his pavement maze in the USA's Norton Museum of Art and his world record-breaking cornfield mazes which extend to an area of nearly 400,000 square feet!

The highly ingenious maze puzzles he has put together for this book are designed to bewilder and deceive. Part of the surprise is that many of them appear deceptively simple. They will tempt you down dead ends and trip you up at every corner! But persevere...

... the ultimate satisfaction of finding your way through a maze is definitely worth all the hard work en route. And remember - some mazes have bridges, which you can either go under or across, to help you on your way.

Enjoy them in any order!

THE RUSSBOROUGH MAZE

Find your way from the entrance to
the inner square of this Irish maze.

See page 73 for solution

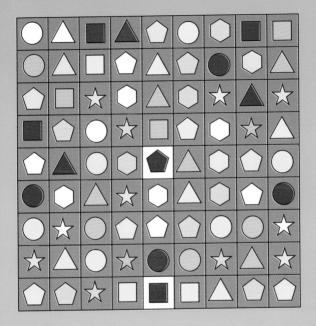

SHAPES MAZE

Starting at the red square on the bottom row, move any direction one square at a time, changing either shape or colour each time, in order to get to the red pentagon in the centre. See page 73 for solution

DELPHIC TEMPLE MAZE

Starting at the arrow, find your way to the centre
of the triangular facade at the top of the maze.

See page 71 for solution

4

THE HATFIELD MAZE

Find your way through this maze, that was planted in 1846 in one of Queen Elizabeth I's favourite palace gardens. Start at the arrow and finish up at the other side of the maze. See page 71 for solution

THE PATCHWORK QUILT MAZE

Moving from shape to shape, find the repeated three colour sequence which will take you from one side of this maze to the other, or from top to bottom. You must not jump shapes and you must finish with the third colour of the sequence at the opposite side. See page 73 for solution

6

START

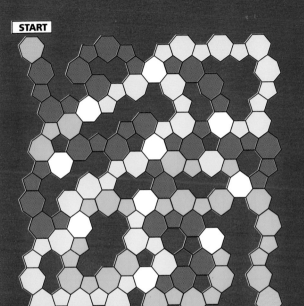

FINISH

SERPENT MAZE

Find your way from "Start" to "Finish", keep to the
same path colour until you reach a white cell;
when you must change path colour.

See page 73 for solution

CELTIC DRAGONS MAZE

Find your way from the entrance to the centre of the
maze, using the bridges en route to help. Escape via
the quick exit bridge. See page 71 for solution

8

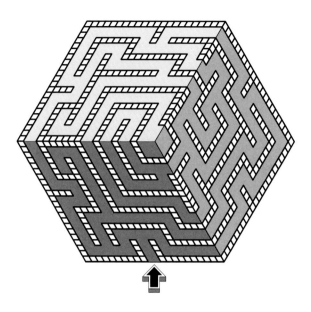

THE CUBE MAZE

Don't be put off by the 3D effect – just follow
the path to the centre of the hexagon.

See page 71 for solution

9

GIANT BRIDGE MAZE

Starting at the green square, change path colour
at each junction (white square) in the repeated
sequence Red – Blue – Yellow – Green to get to the
blue square. You may use paths that pass over or
under the giant bridge. See page 74 for solution

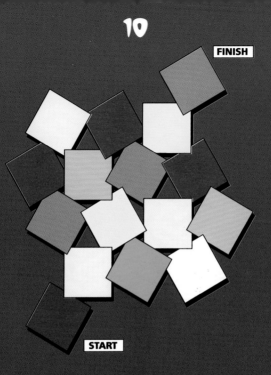

FINISH

START

TILE MAZE

Each of these tiles is either laid over its neighbour
or under it. Travel from the "Start" tile to the "Finish" tile
by alternating from an overlaid tile to an underlaid tile etc.

See page 74 for solution

11

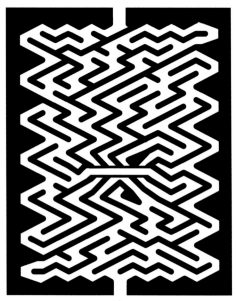

ZIG ZAG MAZE

Use the bridge in the centre to help you
find your way through this maze.

See page 72 for solution

MAZE OF THE PLANETS

**Find your way from the entrance
to the centre of the maze.**

See page 72 for solution

ASTEROID MAZE

The cells in this maze have short (S) and
long (L) sides. Travel from the bottom to the top,
from cell to cell, crossing the boundaries in the
sequence SLL, SLL etc. See page 74 for solution

14

KNIGHT'S DICE MAZE

Starting from the bottom middle square, move
from dice to dice in the repeated sequence
1-2-3-4-5 by jumping like a knight in chess (two
along and one sideways). See page 74 for solution

NOAH'S ARK MAZE

Find your way from the entrance to the centre of the
maze (black dot) and out via the quick exit bridge.

See page 72 for solution

16

GLENDURGAN MAZE

Starting at the arrow find the quickest way to the centre.

See page 72 for solution

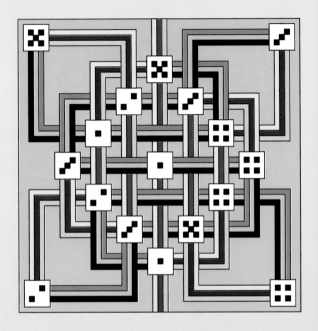

FIRE AND WATER MAZE

The maze consists of fire (red) and water (blue) paths. Enter on the bottom fire path and exit on the top fire path. Each time you reach a dice, you must change from fire to water or from water to fire. Keep a running score of the dice numbers that you pass and try to solve the maze with a score of 33. See page 77 for solution

18

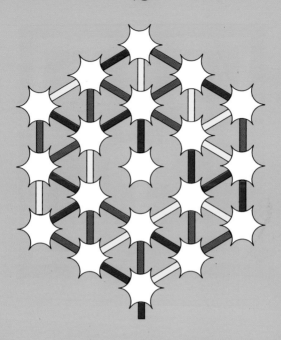

SNOWFLAKE MAZE

Move from star to star, following paths
in the repeated colour sequence
red – blue – yellow, to reach the central star.

See page 77 for solution

19

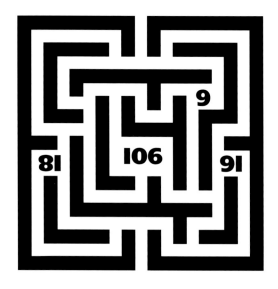

THE FORTY MAZE

**Find a way through this maze
achieving a total of precisely 40.**

See page 75 for solution

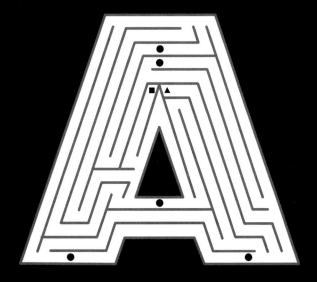

Amazing maze

Starting at the square, travel to the triangle,
passing each of the black dots en route.
No path can be used more than once.

See page 75 for solution

REPTILE MAZE

Starting at the arrow, keep to the
yellow and white paths, in and out
of the reptile's body, to reach the head.

See page 77 for solution

QUEEN'S MAZE

Start at the central bottom square with the "5" on it and jump horizontally, vertically or diagonally, the number of squares indicated by the number on the square. The objective is to find your way to the zero in the centre.

See page 77 for solution

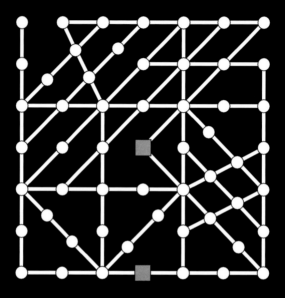

JUMPING·IN·THREES MAZE

Starting at the bottom middle square,
move three nodes at a time in a straight
line to get to the centre square.

See page 75 for solution

VILLA PISANI MAZE

Find your way from the arrow to the inner circle.

See page 75 for solution

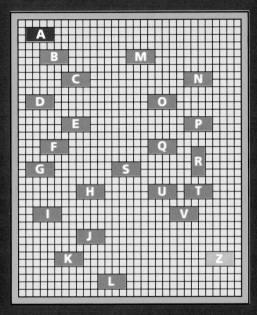

ALPHABET MAZE

In this maze you have 23 squares labelled with letters of the alphabet. Start at A and find your way to Z moving only to those squares that are directly left, right, above or below the current square. E.g. you can move from A to B but not from C to D. You must visit every square once – and only once – en route!

See page 78 for solution

TEN-POINTED STAR MAZE

Starting from the bottom middle square,
find your way to the centre of the maze by
changing path colour at each square.

See page 78 for solution

27

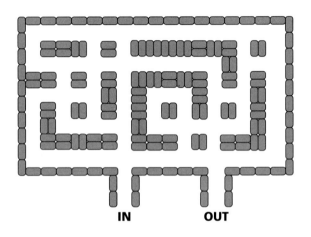

IN　　　　　**OUT**

THE JAMMED TRACTOR MAZE

Imagine you are in a tractor. The steering is jammed
and you can only travel straight or turn left.
You cannot turn right. Find your way through
the maze from "In" to "Out". See page 76 for solution

28

GREEN MAN MAZE

Start at the white square and find
your way to the central white dot
without going over any of the arrows.

See page 76 for solution

THE RAINBOW MAZE

Enter the maze on the bottom red path. Each time you reach a white square, you must change path colour in the repeated sequence red – blue – yellow – green. Your goal is the central square. See page 78 for solution

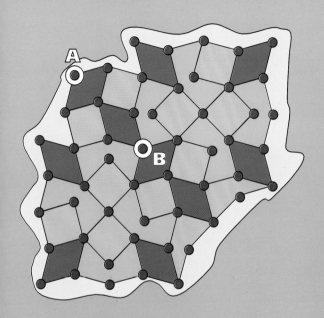

ODD MILEAGE MAZE

Each town (red circle) on this island is exactly one mile from the next town. Find a way of getting from the coastal town (A) to the inland city (B) by travelling an odd number of miles and without retracing any part of your journey en route. See page 78 for solution

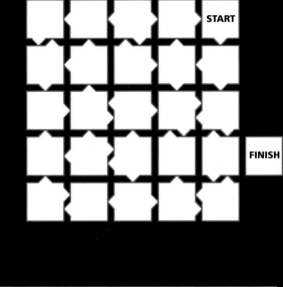

START

FINISH

SQUARE ROUTES MAZE

Find your way from the start box to the finish box.
You may only travel horizontally or vertically in the
directions indicated by the arrows, but you may move any
number of boxes. See page 76 for solution

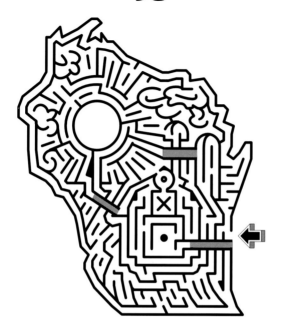

WISCONSIN MAZE

Find your way from the entrance to the
centre of the barn, using the bridges en route
to help. Escape via the quick exit bridge.

See page 76 for solution

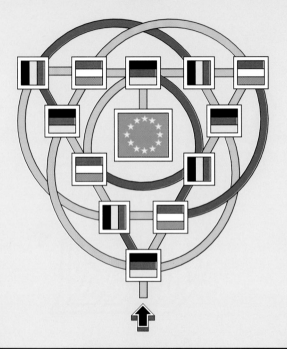

FLAG MAZE

This maze contains the flags of three different countries: Germany, Belgium and The Netherlands. Each time you reach a different flag, you change path colour. The object is to reach the European flag in the centre.

See page 81 for solution

GIANT SNOWFLAKE MAZE

**Move from star to star, following paths
in the repeated colour sequence
green – blue – yellow, to reach the central star.**

See page 81 for solution

35

Prime numbers under 100 are:
2,3,5,7,11,13,17,19,23,29,31,37,41,43,47,53,59,61,
67,71,73,79,83,89,97.

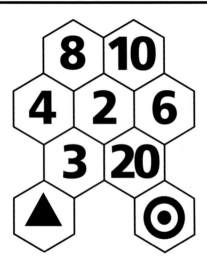

HONEYCOMB MAZE

Travel from the triangle to the circle, keep a running
total which must always be a prime number. You may not
ping-pong backwards and forwards between any two cells.
Obtain the highest possible score under 100 – what is it?

See page 79 for solution

DIAMOND MAZE

Starting at the arrow, find the quickest way to the centre.

See page 79 for solution

37

THE THROOP MAZE

In this maze, each blue dot represents a separate
junction, where you can opt to turn right or left.
The maze has two easily remembered methods of being
solved. What are they? See page 81 for solution

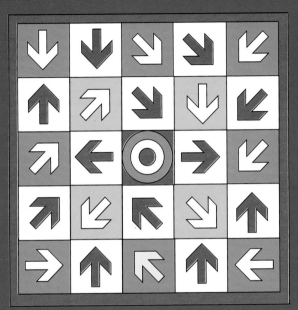

THE 24 ARROWS MAZE

Starting with the yellow arrow, find your way to the central target. Move any distance in the direction indicated. Whenever you stop, change direction as indicated by the next arrow.

See page 81 for solution

ARLEY HALL MAZE

Find the quickest way to the hexagon
at the centre of this maze.

See page 79 for solution

LOCOMOTIVE MAZE

Find your way from the entrance to the nose
of the train and out via the quick exit bridge.

See page 79 for solution

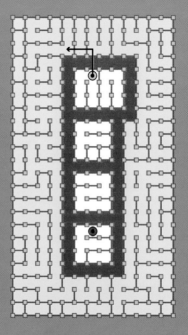

ANTI-MAZE

Go from the green dot to the red dot by moving from grid cell to adjacent grid cell. In each move you must travel through a wall. Unlike the more common path mazes, you cannot travel through empty spaces.

See page 82 for solution

42

STAR-STRUCK MAZE

Find the repeated three colour sequence which will take you from star 1, to star 2 then on to star 3 and back to star 1, moving from one coloured shape to another which shares a boundary.

See page 82 for solution

43

MYTHICAL DRAGON'S MAZE

Find your way from the entrance to the centre
of the maze (the dragon's eye), using the bridges en
route to help. Escape via the quick exit bridge.

See page 80 for solution

44

THE SAXON MAZE

Enter the left-hand side entrance and follow
the route to the centre of the maze, before
taking the quick exit route home.

See page 80 for solution

UFO MAZE

Starting at the arrow, find your way to the centre of the flying saucer. Bridges take paths over and under each other. There is also a quick exit bridge.

See page 82 for solution

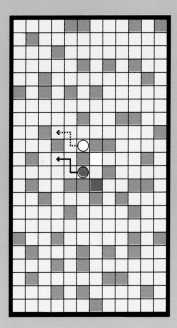

THE TANDEM MAZE

The object in this maze is to manoeuvre the red and the white circles onto the red and white squares. You cannot land on the blue squares and the two circles must always be moved together and kept exactly the same distance apart at all times. See page 82 for solution

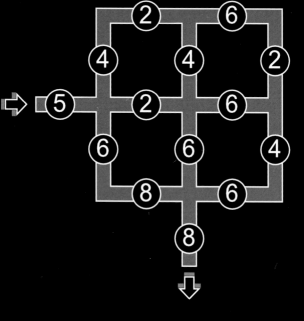

THE WINDOW MAZE

As you move through this maze, keep adding to your running total. Each time this score must be a prime number. Keep moving forward – no doubling back. Finish on a prime number – what is the lowest score you can achieve through the maze? See page 80 for solution

THE MANNINGFORD MAZE

**Find your way through this maze from
bottom to top, via the centre of the maze.**

See page 80 for solution

49

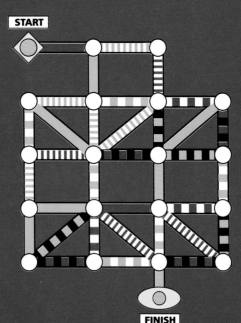

START

FINISH

CONNECTIONS MAZE

From the start, move from junction to
junction, changing either path pattern or
colour each time – but not both – in order to get
to the finish. See page 85 for solution

THE EGYPTIAN FALCON MAZE

Moving from shape to shape, find one repeated three-colour sequence which will take you from one side of this maze to the other, and another from top to bottom. You can travel between shapes if they touch, even if only at a point. Finish with the third colour of the sequence at the opposite side. See page 85 for solution

51

SAFARI MAZE

Start in the middle of the maze and, travelling in
the direction of the spears, pass through each of the
16 intersections without retracing your steps.

See page 83 for solution

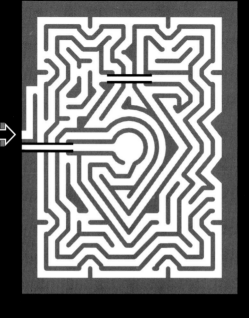

PLAYING CARD MAZE

Find your way from the arrow to the centre of
this maze and out via the quick exit route.

See page 83 for solution

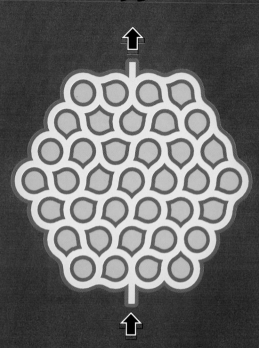

HEXAGONAL ROLLER MAZE

**Travel from the bottom of this maze
to the top, making sure you always move
smoothly forward along the paths.**

See page 85 for solution

54

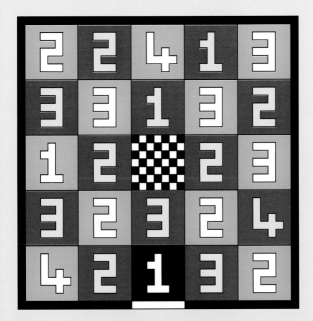

ROOK'S MAZE

Start at the square with the "1" on it in the centre of the
bottom row, and jump forwards, sideways, or backwards,
but never diagonally, the number of squares indicated
by the number on the square. The objective is to find your
way to the central square. See page 85 for solution

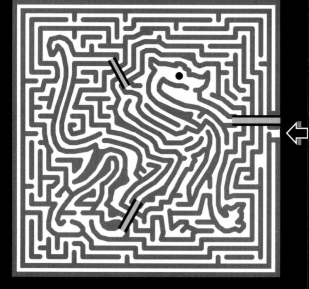

ORIENTAL DRAGON'S MAZE

Find your way from the entrance to the centre
of the maze (dragon's eye), using the bridges en route
to help. Escape via the quick exit bridge.

See page 83 for solution

56

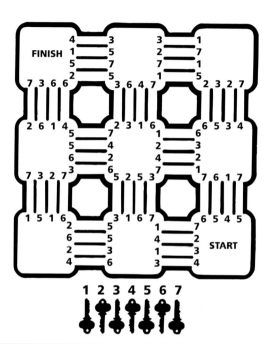

1 2 3 4 5 6 7

KEY DECISION MAZE

The numbered keys above unlock the doors at either
end of the corridors, which join the rooms, in this
maze. Find your way from the room at the bottom
right of the maze to the room at the top left with the
help of only three keys. See page 83 for solution

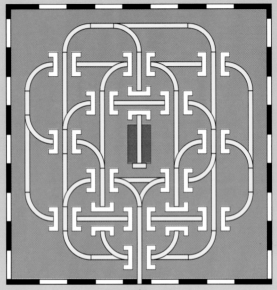

ONE-WAY RAILWAY MAZE

Starting at the arrow, proceed forwards only, over and under the bridges. Your goal is the central station.

See page 85 for solution

58

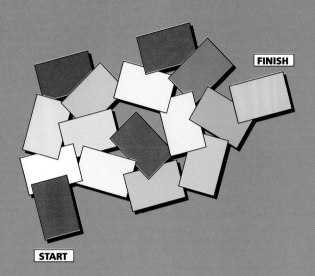

FINISH

START

UPSTAIRS DOWNSTAIRS MAZE

Each of these sheets is either laid over its neighbour
or under it. Travel alternately Upstairs and Downstairs
between the sheets from the "Start" to the "Finish".

See page 86 for solution

LEEDS CASTLE MAZE

Find your way to the centre of this maze, which can be found at Leeds Castle in Kent, England.

See page 84 for solution

VERONICA'S MAZE

Travel through this one-way maze from
the entrance to the centre, always moving smoothly
forwards along the paths.

See page 84 for solution

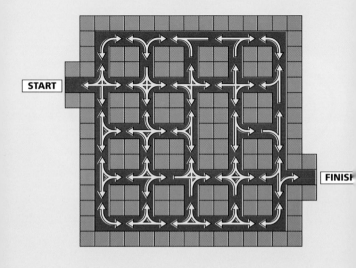

START

FINISH

FARMER'S MAZE

Find your way from Start to Finish by travelling
any number of squares in a straight horizontal or
vertical line. The arrows indicate the direction in
which you must travel. E.g. at the start you can go left
or straight on. You cannot turn right. See page 86 for solution

CREATION MAZE

From one of the two entrances, travel through each apple once and reach the red star without using any path more than once. You can only achieve this from one of the two entrances. See page 86 for solution

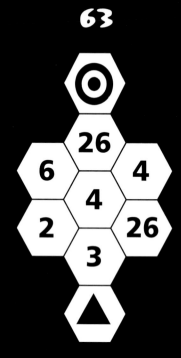

PRIME NUMBER MAZE

From the triangle move from cell to cell to the
circle. At every move, your running total must
be a prime number. You must not return immediately
to the cell you have just left. Finish with a score of 97.

See page 84 for solution

ITALIANATE MAZE

Find your way from the arrow to the centre.

See page 84 for solution

FREEWAY MAZE

Travel through the freeways from start to finish without going over any of the circles.

See page 87 for solution

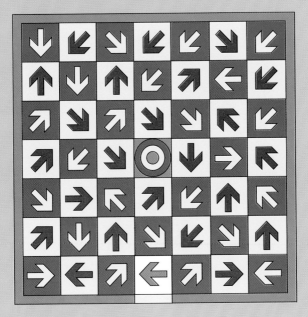

THE 48 ARROWS MAZE

Starting at the arrow in the white square, find your way to the central target. Move any distance in the direction indicated. Whenever you stop, change direction as indicated by the arrow on which you land.

See page 87 for solution

DOLPHIN MAZE

**Starting from the top dolphin's fin trace
a path to the eye of the central dolphin.**

See page 88 for solution

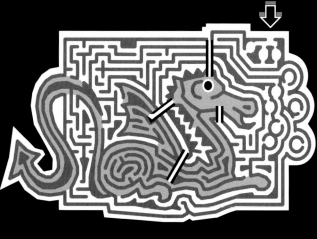

TULLEY'S DRAGON MAZE

Find the quickest way to the dragon's eye and out via the quick exit bridge.

See page 88 for solution

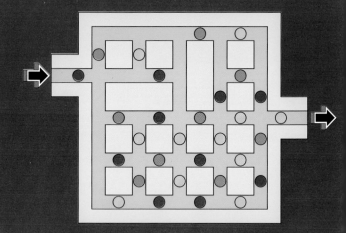

THE MARBLE MAZE

Travel through the maze, from left to right, passing the coloured marbles in the repeated sequence red – green – blue.

See page 86 for solution

LEMON TREE MAZE

Move smoothly forward through this maze, from the trunk to the tip of the tree.

See page 86 for solution

DELPHIC TEMPLE MAZE

THE HATFIELD MAZE

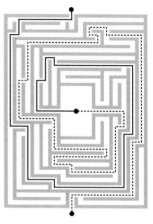

THE CUBE MAZE

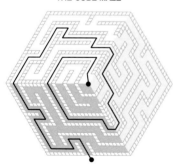

CELTIC DRAGONS MAZE

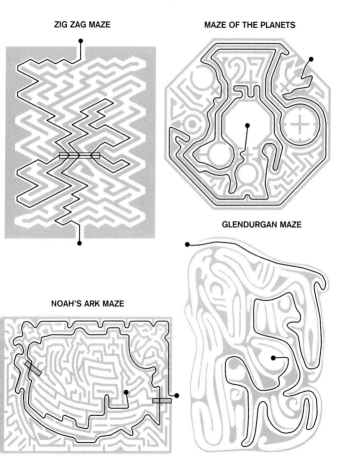

ZIG ZAG MAZE

MAZE OF THE PLANETS

GLENDURGAN MAZE

NOAH'S ARK MAZE

THE RUSSBOROUGH MAZE

SHAPES MAZE

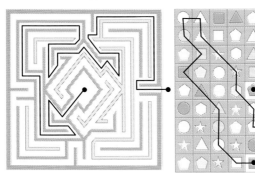

THE PATCHWORK QUILT MAZE

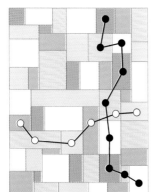

SERPENT MAZE

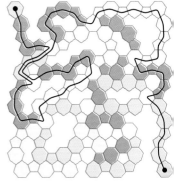

GIANT BRIDGE MAZE

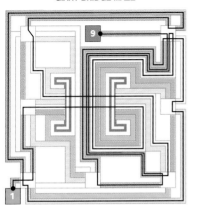

TILE MAZE

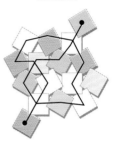

KNIGHT'S DICE MAZE

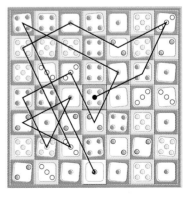

ASTEROID MAZE

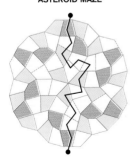

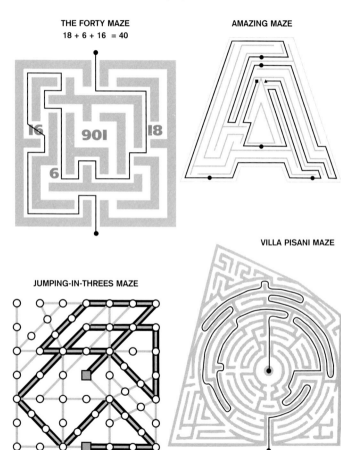

THE FORTY MAZE
18 + 6 + 16 = 40

AMAZING MAZE

JUMPING-IN-THREES MAZE

VILLA PISANI MAZE

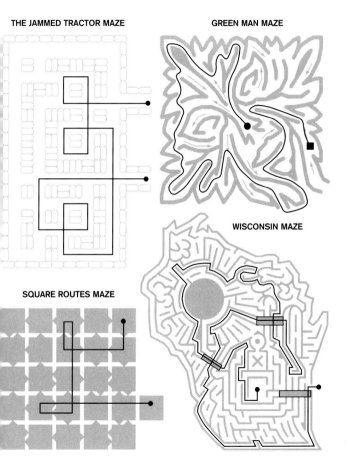

THE JAMMED TRACTOR MAZE

GREEN MAN MAZE

WISCONSIN MAZE

SQUARE ROUTES MAZE

"

FIRE AND WATER MAZE

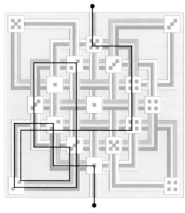

SNOWFLAKE MAZE

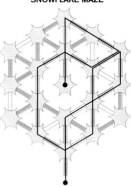

REPTILE MAZE

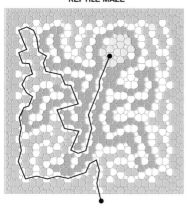

QUEEN'S MAZE

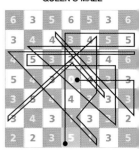

ALPHABET MAZE

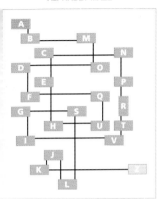

ODD MILEAGE MAZE

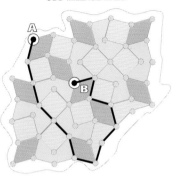

TEN-POINTED STAR MAZE

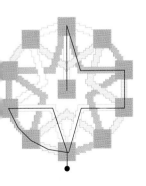

THE RAINBOW MAZE

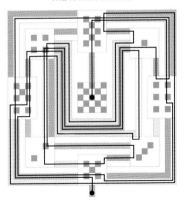

79

HONEYCOMB MAZE
The highest possible score is 79

DIAMOND MAZE

ARLEY HALL MAZE

LOCOMOTIVE MAZE

80

MYTHICAL DRAGON'S MAZE

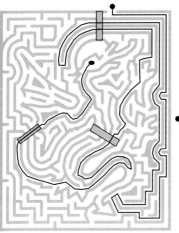

THE MANNINGFORD MAZE

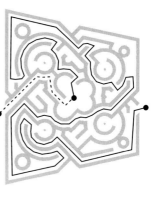

THE SAXON MAZE

THE WINDOW MAZE

The lowest score is 61

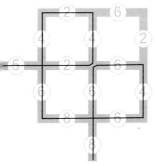

FLAG MAZE

GIANT SNOWFLAKE MAZE

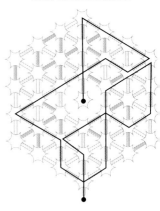

THE THROOP MAZE
(One solution is turn left and right alternately at each junction, the other solution is to turn right and left alternately at each junction)

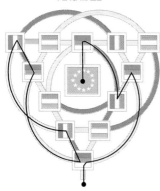

THE 24 ARROWS MAZE

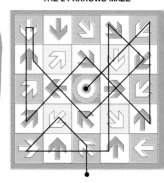

82

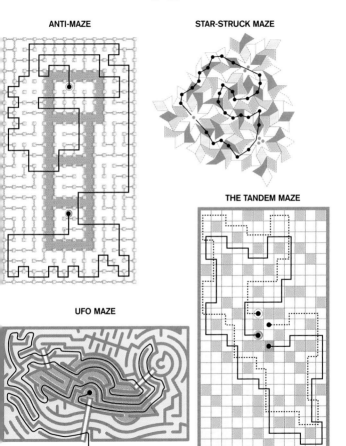

ANTI-MAZE

STAR-STRUCK MAZE

THE TANDEM MAZE

UFO MAZE

83

KEY DECISION MAZE

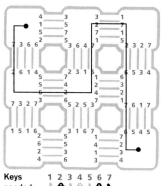

Keys needed: 2, 6 and 7

PLAYING CARD MAZE

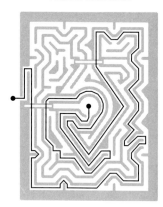

ORIENTAL DRAGON'S MAZE

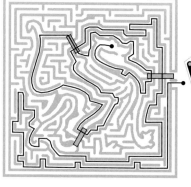

SAFARI MAZE

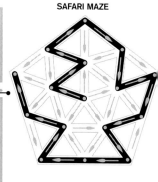

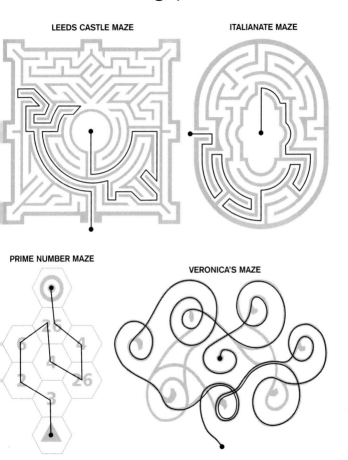

LEEDS CASTLE MAZE

ITALIANATE MAZE

PRIME NUMBER MAZE

VERONICA'S MAZE

HEXAGONAL ROLLER MAZE

THE EGYPTIAN FALCON MAZE

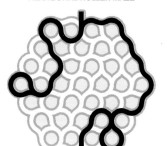

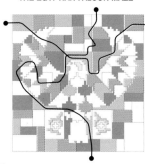

CONNECTIONS MAZE

START

FINISH

ONE-WAY RAILWAY MAZE

ROOK'S MAZE

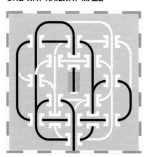

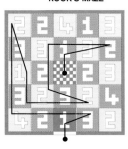

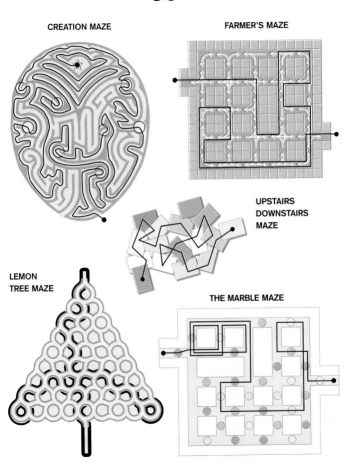

CREATION MAZE

FARMER'S MAZE

UPSTAIRS
DOWNSTAIRS
MAZE

LEMON
TREE MAZE

THE MARBLE MAZE

87

FREEWAY MAZE

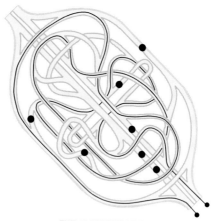

THE 48 ARROWS MAZE

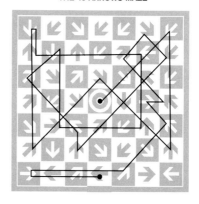

88

DOLPHIN MAZE

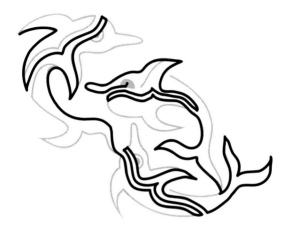

TULLEY'S DRAGON MAZE

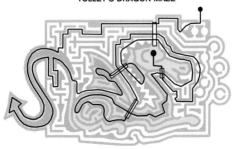

HISTORY OF MAZES

Mazes go back in history to at least 2,000 years BC. Until the 11th century, they were single path labyrinths, which were used not as puzzles but for ritual walking and processions.

The labyrinth motif from Greek mythology appears to have been used in mosaic pavements throughout the Roman Empire. While in Scandinavia, over 600 stone labyrinths line the shore of the Baltic Sea. Many are said to have been built by fishermen who walked through them before embarking on fishing trips. Their aim was to lead evil spirits into the labyrinth and to abandon them there, confused, whilst they set off to sea!

In 13th century France, medieval Christian pavement mazes were laid in the stone floors of gothic cathedrals, with names such as Chemin de Jerusalem reflecting the recent crusades. Then in the Middle Ages, formal gardens were established throughout

Europe and puzzle hedge mazes became an amusement of kings and princes. The Dutch in particular were keen on hedge mazes and in 1690, King William III built the famous hedge maze at Hampton Court Palace having created an earlier one in 1682 at Het Loo Palace in Holland.

In Victorian times, dozens of new hedge mazes were built in parks for the general public's amusement and the nobility added mazes to their gardens. This British enthusiasm for mazes spread through the English speaking world and mazes gained popularity as far afield as Australia and the United States.

In the 20th century, the two world wars caused gardens to be neglected. Many mazes were irretrievably lost but along with the upsurge of mass leisure, travel and tourism in the 70s, interest in mazes has been renewed and more are being built around the world today than at any other time in history!

**A special thank-you to all the
maze specialists who very kindly
contributed to this book:**

**All mazes were compiled/designed by Adrian
Fisher, except for the mazes by the following
contributors...**

Robert Abbott
(Marble Maze, Connections Maze, Farmer's Maze)

Randoll Coate
(Creation Maze)

Scott Kim
(The Tandem Maze, Anti-Maze, Alphabet Maze)

Ed Pegg
(Asteroid Maze, Upstairs Downstairs Maze,
The Window Maze)

Steve Ryan
(Amazing Maze, Key Decision Maze, Square Routes
Maze, Safari Maze, Freeway Maze)